CW00544139

by Iain Gray

Lang**Syne**

PUBLISHING

WRITING *to* REMEMBER

Lang**Syne**

PUBLISHING

WRITING *to* REMEMBER

79 Main Street, Newtongrange,
Midlothian EH22 4NA
Tel: 0131 344 0414   Fax: 0845 075 6085
E-mail: info@lang-syne.co.uk
www.langsyneshop.co.uk

Design by Dorothy Meikle
Printed by Printwell Ltd
© Lang Syne Publishers Ltd 2018

ISBN 978-1-85217-114-8

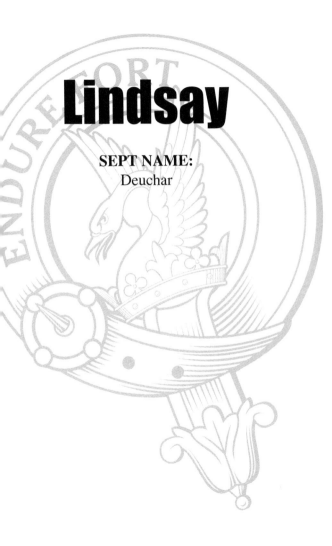

Lindsay

SEPT NAME:
Deuchar

Lindsay

MOTTO:
Endure with strength.

CREST:
A swan with a coronet.

TERRITORY:
Angus.

Chapter one:

The origins of the clan system

by Rennie McOwan

The original Scottish clans of the Highlands and the great families of the Lowlands and Borders were gatherings of families, relatives, allies and neighbours for mutual protection against rivals or invaders.

Scotland experienced invasion from the Vikings, the Romans and English armies from the south. The Norman invasion of what is now England also had an influence on land-holding in Scotland. Some of these invaders stayed on and in time became 'Scottish'.

The word clan derives from the Gaelic language term 'clann', meaning children, and it was first used many centuries ago as communities were formed around tribal lands in glens and mountain fastnesses.

The format of clans changed over the centuries, but at its best the chief and his family held the land on behalf of all, like trustees, and the ordinary clansmen and women believed they had a blood relationship with the founder of their clan.

There were two way duties and obligations. An inadequate chief could be deposed and replaced by someone of greater ability.

Clan people had an immense pride in race. Their relationship with the chief was like adult children to a father and they had a real dignity.

The concept of clanship is very old and a more feudal notion of authority gradually crept in.

Pictland, for instance, was divided into seven principalities ruled by feudal leaders who were the strongest and most charismatic leaders of their particular groups.

By the sixth century the 'British' kingdoms of Strathclyde, Lothian and Celtic Dalriada (Argyll) had emerged and Scotland, as one nation, began to take shape in the time of King Kenneth MacAlpin.

Some chiefs claimed descent from

ancient kings which may not have been accurate in every case.

By the twelfth and thirteenth centuries the clans and families were more strongly brought under the central control of Scottish monarchs.

Lands were awarded and administered more and more under royal favour, yet the power of the area clan chiefs was still very great.

The long wars to ensure Scotland's independence against the expansionist ideas of English monarchs extended the influence of some clans and reduced the lands of others.

Those who supported Scotland's greatest king, Robert the Bruce, were awarded the territories of the families who had opposed his claim to the Scottish throne.

In the Scottish Borders country – the notorious Debatable Lands – the great families built up a ferocious reputation for providing warlike men accustomed to raiding into England and occasionally fighting one another.

Chiefs had the power to dispense justice and to confiscate lands and clan warfare produced a society where martial virtues – courage, hardiness, tenacity – were greatly admired.

Gradually the relationship between the clans and the Crown became strained as Scottish monarchs became more orientated to life in the Lowlands and, on occasion, towards England.

The Highland clans spoke a different language, Gaelic, whereas the language of Lowland Scotland and the court was Scots and in more modern times, English.

Highlanders dressed differently, had different customs, and their wild mountain land sometimes seemed almost foreign to people living in the Lowlands.

It must be emphasised that Gaelic culture was very rich and story-telling, poetry, piping, the clarsach (harp) and other music all flourished and were greatly respected.

Highland culture was different from other parts of Scotland but it was not inferior or less sophisticated.

Central Government, whether in London or Edinburgh, sometimes saw the Gaelic clans as

*"The spirit of the clan means much
to thousands of people"*

a challenge to their authority and some sent
expeditions into the Highlands and west to crush
the power of the Lords of the Isles.

Nevertheless, when the eighteenth century
Jacobite Risings came along the cause of the
Stuarts was mainly supported by Highland clans.

The word Jacobite comes from the Latin
for James – Jacobus. The Jacobites wanted to
restore the exiled Stuarts to the throne of Britain.

The monarchies of Scotland and England
became one in 1603 when King James VI of
Scotland (1st of England) gained the English
throne after Queen Elizabeth died.

The Union of Parliaments of Scotland and
England, the Treaty of Union, took place in 1707.

Some Highland clans, of course, and
Lowland families opposed the Jacobites and
supported the incoming Hanoverians.

After the Jacobite cause finally went down
at Culloden in 1746 a kind of ethnic cleansing took
place. The power of the chiefs was curtailed.
Tartan and the pipes were banned in law.

Many emigrated, some because they

wanted to, some because they were evicted by force. In addition, many Highlanders left for the cities of the south to seek work.

Many of the clan lands became home to sheep and deer shooting estates.

But the warlike traditions of the clans and the great Lowland and Border families lived on, with their descendants fighting bravely for freedom in two world wars.

Remember the men from whence you came, says the Gaelic proverb, and to that could be added the role of many heroic women.

The spirit of the clan, of having roots, whether Highland or Lowland, means much to thousands of people.

*Clan warfare produced a society where
courage and tenacity were greatly admired*

Chapter two:

In royal favour

Recipients of honours and titles that include the premier earldom of Scotland, the Lindsays have produced a memorable array of sons and daughters who have gained both fame and infamy.

Their roots lie with those Norman knights who accompanied William, Duke of Normandy, on his invasion of England in 1066 and who in later decades found a home in Scotland.

One possible derivation of their name is that it stems from 'Lindsey', meaning 'Lincoln's Island', a district in Lincolnshire, while another explanation is that it derives from 'the island of the lime tree.'

Walter Lindsay was a member of the council of Prince David, Earl of Huntingdon, and it is likely he was invited to Scotland sometime after the prince became King of Scots in 1124.

One of his descendants subsequently acquired the lands of Crawford, in Upper Clydesdale.

By 1285 the Lindsays appear to have been very firmly in the royal favour, as Sir John Lindsay, Great Chamberlain of Scotland, was granted a charter by King Alexander III to hold the lands of Wauchope, in Dumfriesshire, as a barony.

In 1494, however, the 12th Laird of Wauchope was forfeited by the Crown for his part in Borders pillage and slaughter. Some parts of the land were later regained, and Lindsays remained lairds until about the close of the seventeenth century.

Crawford Castle, in Upper Clydesdale, was the main seat of the family, and a tower on the site known as Tower Lindsay was successfully stormed by the great freedom fighter William Wallace during the Wars of Independence and the occupying English garrison put to the sword.

A landmark date in the history of the

Crawfords is 1398, when Sir David Lindsay of Crawford was created Earl of Crawford.

An earlier fourteenth century marriage to an heiress of the great earldom of Angus had brought the Lindsays vast landholdings in this rich and fertile territory, particularly those of Glenesk and Edzell.

Angus became their principal territory through time, with Finavon, at the mouth of the Angus glens, as their main seat. This branch of the family became known as the Crawford-Lindsays.

Recognised as the premier earldom of Scotland, the earldom of Crawford was followed by the granting of the earldom of Lindsay to a branch of the family in 1633 and the earldom of Balcarres to another branch in 1651.

The Lindsays also held the Haddingtonshire barony of the Byres, and it is from this branch of the family that the renowned line of the Lindsays of the Byres and the Earls of Lindsay were descended.

In 1541 the 8th Earl of Crawford was

seized by his sons Alexander, the Master of Crawford, and his brother, John, and unceremoniously manacled and thrown into confinement.

Understandably indignant over the outrage he disinherited his sons, who were found guilty of 'constructive parricide' and outlawed.

The earl accordingly made provision for his estates and honours to go to his next male heir, who was his cousin Sir David Lindsay of Edzell and Glenesk.

Sir David became the 9th Earl of Crawford, but on his death he restored the title to the son of the 'Wicked Master' of Crawford, with the important proviso that should this line fail, the earldom should return to the male heirs of Edzell and Glenesk

The Crawford-Lindsay line failed in 1808, but it was not until forty years later, following a judgement of the House of Lords, that his wish was fulfilled when the earldoms of Crawford and Balcarres were united.

The Earl of Crawford and Balcarres is today recognised as Chief of the Clan Lindsay.

Although the Lindsays recognise a close link with the equally renowned Crawford family, through a marriage in the twelfth century of a Lindsay to a Crawford woman, the Crawford family is officially recognised as a distinct family and not, as some claim, a sept of the Lindsays.

The confusion has arisen because the Crawfords, before acquiring their main lands in Ayrshire, had also at one time held the lands of Crawford in Upper Clydesdale.

Known as the 'lightsome Lindsays' because of their reputation for cheerfulness, the Lindsays were nevertheless involved in many grim and bloody incidents.

Martial valour appears to have been a strong family trait, and as early as 1268 Sir David Lindsay of Crawford and the Byres was one of several knights who died while on Crusade to the Holy Land.

Sir John Lindsay was one of the six trusted barons of the realm who swore to acknowledge the infant Maid of Norway as

successor in 1289 to Alexander III, while Sir
Thomas Lindsay of Crawford was one of the
nobles who in 1320 signed the famous clarion
call of Scotland's independence known as the
Declaration of Arbroath.

Sir Ralph Lindsay fought on the side of
the great warrior king Robert the Bruce at the
battle of Bannockburn in 1314, after earlier
supporting the rapacious cause of the English
monarch, Edward I, known as the Hammer of
the Scots.

According to legend, Sir Ralph resolved
to reform his life after seeing a vision of St.
Cuthbert. His brother, however, Sir Simon
Lindsay, took the side of the English and was
forfeited by Bruce after his victory at
Bannockburn.

His son, Sir John Lindsay, restored his
family's honour by fighting to the death at
the side of his fellow Scots at the battle
of Neville's Cross, near Durham, in
Northumberland, in 1346.

The Scots king, David II, who had also

fought bravely, was captured and held prisoner in England for eleven years.

Nearly forty years later, in 1384, Sir Alexander Lindsay of Glenesk played a daring role in attempting to repulse an invasion of Scotland launched by John of Gaunt, the Duke of Lancaster.

Sir Alexander captured one of the English ships that had landed near Queensferry, putting the entire crew to the sword.

Chapter three:

Knightly valour

It was in 1388 that Sir James Lindsay of Crawford achieved noble fame after helping to turn the tide of battle at Otterburn as the Scottish commander, James, the 2nd Earl of Douglas, lay mortally wounded on the field.

The Scots had earlier been involved in a skirmish outside the walls of Newcastle when the young Earl of Douglas managed to snatch the silk pennant from the lance of his adversary Henry Percy, heir to the 1st Earl of Northumberland and better known to posterity as Henry Hotspur.

Douglas proceeded to lead his army back towards Scotland, but Hotspur, stung by the insult to his honour, swore his precious pennant would never be allowed to cross the border.

He pursued Douglas, and the two armies clashed at Otterburn, the young earl receiving a fatal blow.

As the Scots army faltered, demoralised over the fate of their commander, Sir James Lindsay knelt by his side and asked him how he fared, to which Douglas replied 'dying in my armour, as my fathers have done, thank God!'

On Douglas's dying command, Lindsay raised the famed Banner of the Bloody Heart of the Douglases, rallied the Scots, and led them to victory.

The Lindsays performed further deeds of knightly valour, most notably in 1390 when Sir David Lindsay of Glenesk, one of the most famous knights of his age, took part in a famed tournament on London Bridge.

The young Sir David had been at a banquet at which Lord Welles, the English ambassador to Scotland, had boasted of the superiority of English knights and issued Sir David with the challenge 'if you know not the chivalry and valiant deeds of Englishmen, appoint me a day and place where you choose and you shall have experience.'

Sir David readily accepted the challenge

and the long and broad expanse of the bridge spanning the Thames was chosen as the venue for the joust.

On their first 'tilt' at one another, Sir David managed to stay in his saddle despite his helmet being struck a mighty blow by Lord Welles's lance.

The partisan English onlookers, much in the same way as football fans may object to a goal scored against their team, clamoured that Sir David was guilty of cheating because he was tied to his saddle.

The Scots knight dismounted and then, unaided, hoisted himself and his cumbersome armour back into the saddle, demonstrating he had not been bound to his saddle, and proceeded to knock his opponent to the ground – disproving his haughty boast of the superiority of English knighthood.

Sir David Lindsay was also among a number of lairds and their followers who in 1391, at Glen Brierachan, bravely attempted to defend the shire of Angus from the ravages of Duncan

Stewart, a son of Alexander, Earl of Buchan, known as the Wolf of Badenoch. A number of lairds were killed and Sir David wounded. It was this Sir David who, in 1398, was created 1st Earl of Crawford.

While Sir David is renowned for his valour, his great grandson gained infamy as the ferocious 'Tiger' Earl of Crawford, also known as 'Earl Beardie' because of the long, unkempt, ginger beard he sported.

The 4th Earl of Crawford, the Tiger not only set himself at bloody odds with his Angus neighbours, but with his monarch, James II. The Tiger's father had been chosen as chief justiciar of Arbroath Abbey, but in 1445 the office was transferred to the rival Ogilvies of Inverquharity.

Taking this as a gross personal insult, the earl marched his men towards the abbey to engage a force of Ogilvies and their supporters. As the battle was about to begin the Tiger's father, the 3rd earl, was killed by an Ogilvie retainer as he attempted to act as peacemaker.

Furious at the loss of his father the Tiger

all but slaughtered the Ogilvie force before burning and ravaging their lands.

The Tiger Earl had also been stung by what he perceived as the degradation of the House of March, of which his wife Elizabeth Dunbar was a daughter, by the Stuart monarchs, and resolved to avenge this by entering into a bond with the Earl of Douglas and the Earl of Ross 'that they should take each other's part in every quarrel and against every man, the king himself not excepted.'

James II managed to crush the rebellion, with the Tiger Earl defeated in 1452 near Brechin by royal forces led by the Earl of Huntly.

The House of Lindsay was only saved from destruction, and the earl himself saved from execution as a traitor, when he appeared before his monarch dressed as a beggar, his feet and head bare, and abjectly apologised for his conduct and begged forgiveness.

The king duly pardoned the earl, and fulfilled an earlier vow he had made that he would 'make the highest stone the lowest' at the earl's castle of Finavon, by throwing a pebble he had found on the battlements from the castle's tower.

The House of Lindsay was saved, but the infamous Tiger Earl died six months later.

His son, David, became the 5th Earl of Crawford and was created Duke of Montrose by James III in 1488, only a few months before his death at the battle of Sauchieburn, near Stirling.

The battle had been fought between the monarch and rebels opposed to his rule. As he fled the battlefield, a mysterious stranger stabbed the king to death.

The 8th Earl of Crawford also fell in battle, this time at the disastrous battle of Flodden in 1513. He fell with his monarch, James IV, while leading part of the Scottish vanguard.

Chapter four:

Courtiers and poets

**Different branches of what had become a
dynasty of Lindsays and related branches took
opposing sides over the cause of the ill-fated
Mary, Queen of Scots.**

One of her loyal courtiers, the 10th Earl of
Crawford, acted as cupbearer at the banquet
following her marriage to Lord Darnley and
remained faithful to her even after her defeat at the
Battle of Langside in 1568.

The 5th Lord Lindsay of the Byres was
one of the nobles into whose care the infant Mary
had been committed in 1542, but Patrick, the 6th
Lord Lindsay of the Byres, was a staunch
adherent of the religious Reformation and an
implacable foe of the Queen.

He took part in the murder of her
secretary David Rizzio at her apartments at
Holyrood, and was one of the Scottish magnates
who bullied her into giving up her crown in

favour of her infant son, the future James VI.

Ludovic, the 16th Earl of Crawford, was known as the 'loyal earl', for his support of the ill-starred Charles I, while the 3rd Earl of Balcarres was a loyal Jacobite who spent 10 years in exile in France following the 'Glorious Revolution' of 1688 that set William of Orange on the thrones of England and Scotland.

The 20th Earl of Crawford, however, proved loyal to the Hanoverian cause at the time of the abortive 1745 Rebellion, holding the Lowlands for the government while the detested Duke of Cumberland, victor of the battle of Culloden in 1746, ravaged the Highlands.

He later commanded Lord Crawford-Lindsay's Highlanders, later to become better known as the Black Watch.

When not engaged on the field of battle the Lindsays and members of cadet branches of the family flourished in a number of rather more peaceful occupations.

One of the most notable was the royal courtier, diplomat, and poet Sir David Lindsay of the Mount, near Cupar, in Fife. Born about 1486, he had a colourful and eventful life that included acting as an usher to the infant and future James V, and the office of Lord Lyon King of Arms of Scotland.

Known as the Poet of the Reformation, he was the author of a satirical drama called *The Three Estates* that was performed before James V and his court in Linlithgow palace in 1540.

An amusing but biting satire of the abuse of power and the lifestyles of the three estates, or classes, of burgesses, lords spiritual, and lords temporal, the play still has a resonance today, and an updated version was staged to great acclaim at the Edinburgh International Festival in 1948.

Robert Lindsay of Pitscottie is remembered as the author of *The Historie and Chronicles of Scotland*, which, if not wholly accurate, is at least colourful, while Lady Anne Lindsay, born in 1750 and the eldest daughter of the 5th Earl of Balcarres, wrote the popular song *Auld Robin Gray*.

In the world of science, James Bowman

Lindsay was a Forfarshire weaver who in 1854 patented a system of telegraphy through wireless, decades before Marconi gained popularity and credit for his own system.

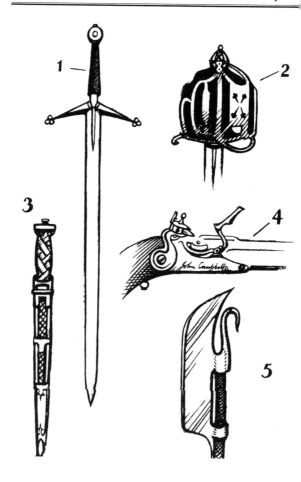

Clan weapons

1) The claymore or two-handed sword
   (fifteenth or early sixteenth century)

2) Basket hilt of broadsword
   made in Stirling, 1716

3) Highland dirk
   (eighteenth century)

4) Steel pistol *(detail)* made in Doune

5) Head of Lochaber Axe as carried
   in the '45 and earlier